ISBN: 9798375112800

Imprint: Independently published

Disclaimer: All answers are correct as of 18th January 2022.

Stenlake Publications presents:

Sunderland A.F.C. Crossword

Check out our other books:

Liverpool Crossword
Manchester United Crossword
Arsenal Crossword
Manchester City Crossword
Tottenham Hotspur Crossword
Chelsea Crossword
Leeds United Crossword
Newcastle United Crossword
Leicester City Crossword
Celtic Crossword
Rangers Crossword
England Crossword

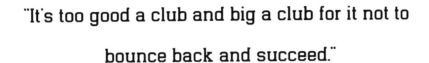

"It's too good a club and big a club for it not to

bounce back and succeed."

- Martin Bain

"I learned my trade at Arsenal, became a footballer at Manchester

City, but Sunderland got under my skin. I love Sunderland."

- Niall Quinn

"I didn't want to entertain other offers. I'm very happy here

and I want to do everything I can to help get the club back

to where I think it belongs."

- Aiden McGeady

[On Charlie Hurley]

"The Greatest Centre Half The World Has Ever Seen"

- Title of the book by author Mark Metcalf

Contents Page

Round 1 - Founding & History

Sunderland and District Teachers A.F.C were founded in 1879 and adopted their current name a year later. They were one of the most successful sides of the early era in English club football. winning six First Division titles and an FA Cup before WWII.

Across

2. Home ground used between 1886 and 1898 which is named after a road that today runs past the Monkwearmouth Hospital. (9.4)

4. Sunderland won the 1936 Charity Shield against this London club. (7)

6. In December 1908. Sunderland beat this team 9-1 to achieve their highest ever league win. (9.6)

7. Young Sunderland goalkeeper who died as a result of being kicked by a Chelsea player after he had picked up the ball following a back pass in 1936. (5.6)

11. Sunderland beat this Scottish team in an 1895 game described as the "World Championship" match. (5.2.10)

13. Joined Sunderland in 1902 and went on to captain the team for ten years. (6.8)

15. The club's founder. (5.5)

16. Scotland international that broke the 30-goal mark for the second consecutive season in 1893 and scored a total of 133 league goals for the club. (4.8)

17. Sunderland's first manager resigned and joined this club in 1896. winning the first of their 19 league titles. (9)

18. All-time record scorer with 228 goals. (5.6)

19. First manager. (3.6)

Down

1. Sunderland won the 1937 FA Cup Final against this team. (7.5.3)

3. Man who is regarded as the founder of the Football League who once declared Sunderland as the "Team of All Talents". (7.8)

5. Sunderland goalkeeper who set a 19th-century record by not conceding in 87 of his 290 top division appearances (30%). (3.4)

8. Captain of Sunderland when they won the 1912/13 league title. (7.7)

9. Nationality of manager Bob Kyle. Sunderland's longest-serving manager. (5)

10. In 1898. Sunderland moved to this ground that would be their home for almost a century. (5.4)

12. Sunderland just escaped relegation from the First Division by one point in the 1927/28 season despite this player scoring 35 goals. (4.8)

13. Sunderland won the 1891/92 league title after defeating this team. nicknamed 'The Villans'. (5.5)

14. After winning the 1891/92 Football League. this newspaper described Sunderland as "a wonderfully fine team". (3.5)

Round 2 - 1950/60s

The late 50s saw a sharp downturn in the club's fortunes as they were involved in a major financial scandal in 1957. The club were relegated the following year for the first time in their 68-year league history. They won promotion back to the First Division six years later but ended the decade back in the Second Division.

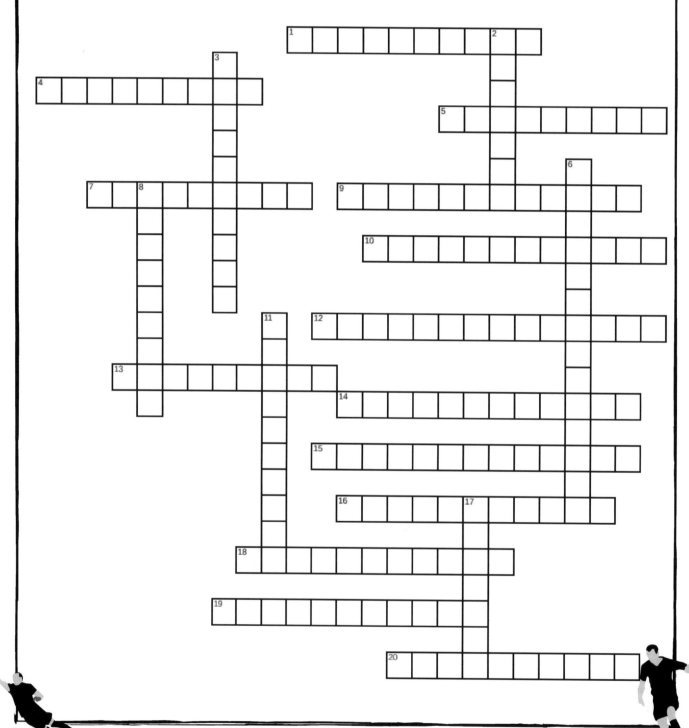

Across

1. England World Cup winner who scored six goals for West Ham against Sunderland in 1968 in an 8-0 defeat. (5.5)

4. Sunderland's first-ever match in the League Cup was a 4-3 defeat to this club. nicknamed 'The Bees' in 1960. (9)

5. In 1967. Sunderland spent the summer in a North American League and were based in this Canadian city under the name _____ Royal Canadians. (9)

7. Manager when they suffered their first-ever relegation in the 1957/58 season. (4.5)

9. Goalkeeper from 1958 to 1968 who made 134 league appearances for the club. (5.7)

10. Midfielder who is fourth on the club's all-time appearance list with 447 appearances before finishing his career at Newcastle and Middlesbrough. (4.8)

12. The club's record League Cup win of 7-1 came against this club. nicknamed 'Latics' in 1962. (6.8)

13. Left-half signed from Rangers in 1965 who is generally regarded as one of Scotland's greatest ever players. (3.6)

14. Midfielder who was the top scorer in the 1967/68 and 1968/69 seasons for the club and would later play for and caretaker manage Newcastle. (5.7)

15. Sunderland were relegated after this East Midlands team failed to beat Birmingham City on the final day of the 1957/58 season. (9.4)

16. Scored 63 goals in 74 games for the club in the early 60s and would later win many honours with Derby County and Nottingham Forest as manager. (5.6)

18. 1960 signing from Birmingham. who was the first player to sign for Sunderland that had played in a European Club final having played in the Inter-Cities Fairs Cup Final in 1960. against Barcelona. (5.6)

19. Birmingham-born forward who was the First Division top scorer in the 1949/50 season with 25 goals. (6.5)

20. Liverpudlian who is second (highest outfielder) on Sunderland's all-time appearance list with 452 between 1957 and 1971. (3.7)

Down

2. Sunderland failed to win promotion to the top-flight in the 1962 season after being unable to beat this Welsh club on the last day of the season. (7)

3. Sunderland broke the British transfer record to sign this Welsh striker for £30,000 in 1950. (6.4)

6. Scotsman nicknamed 'Cannonball Charlie' for his shooting ability who scored 62 league goals in 107 appearances for the club. (7.7)

8. Scottish international goalkeeper Willie Fraser. signed in 1954 was born in this commonwealth nation. (9)

11. Sunderland were knocked out of the 1962/63 League Cup semi-final by this team who went to lose the all-second city final 3-1 on aggregate. (5.5)

17. In September 1955. Sunderland came from 3-0 down to win 4-3 for the only time in their history against this London team. (7)

One the club's finest days came in 1973 as they won their second FA Cup in one of the great underdog stories as a team from the Second Division won the cup for the first time. The victory meant qualification into European competition for the first time. There was not much to cheer about after that apart from a promotion and first League Cup Final as the club were relegated to the third tier for the first time in 1987.

Across

2. Comedian who recorded "Sunderland All The Way" for the 1973 FA Cup Final. (5.7)

3. Opposition for the 1973 FA Cup Final (5.6)

7. Opposition for the 1985 League Cup Final. (7.4)

8. Missed a penalty for Sunderland in the League Cup Final. (5.6)

9. Scored the only goal of the 1973 FA Cup Final. (3.11)

12. Newcastle-born midfielder who made over 400 appearances for the club between 1983 and 1996. (6.9)

14. Captained Sunderland to FA Cup glory and is nicknamed the 'Little General'. (5.4)

15. Had an 8-game spell as caretaker manager at Sunderland in 1987. (4.10)

17. Player signed from Newcastle. known as the "Clown Prince of Soccer" and is generally regarded as one of English football's finest ever entertainers. (3.10)

18. This Newcastle player scored a hat-trick against Sunderland on New Year's Day 1985 before playing for Liverpool as well as winning 59 England caps. (5.9)

Down

1. Sunderland were eliminated from the 1973/74 UEFA Cup Winners' Cup by this Portuguese club. (8.6)

2. Sunderland visited Elland Road in May 1974 to play a testimonial match for this Leeds legend. (5.7)

4. Centre-back who made over 200 appearances for the club in the 70s and won 65 caps for England. (5.6)

5. Sunderland's heroic goalkeeper in the 1973 FA Cup Final. (5.10)

6. Scored a hat-trick against Newcastle at St James' Park in 1979. (4.6)

10. Centre-back signed from Cardiff in 1984 who would go on to make over 350 appearances for the club. (4.7)

11. Scored an own goal in the 1985 Football League Cup Final. (6.8)

13. Sunderland signed this striker from Arsenal in December 1983 but is better known for his time at Sheffield Wednesday and Leeds. (3.7)

15. Sunderland were promoted back to the top division in 1988 under this manager. (5.5)

16. Sunderland beat Vasas Budapest in the 1973/74 UEFA Cup Winners' Cup who are from this nation. (7)

Round 4 - 1990s

This decade started with one of the most unusual promotions back to the top-flight but they only lasted two seasons. The club did reach another FA Cup Final in 1992. again as a Second Division club but were unable to repeat their heroics of '73. The club yo-yo'd through the 90s but ended the decade in the Premier League with a new 42.000-seater stadium.

Across

1. Club that Kevin Ball joined after nine years at Sunderland. (6)

5. Sunderland beat this club in the 1990 Second Division play-off semi-final. (9,6)

8. Appointed as chairman in 1997. (3,6)

11. South Shields-born striker who was top scorer in the 1995/96 promotion-winning season with 14 goals. (5,7)

13. In 1992. Sunderland became the first Second Division side to reach the FA Cup Final since this London team ten years before. (6,4,7)

16. Sunderland signed this former Newcastle and England winger from Bradford in March 1997. (5,6)

17. Manager who led the club to the 1992 FA Cup Final. (7,6)

18. Former Oldham defender who joined Sunderland in 1997 after playing in France and would make over 140 appearances for the club. (5,5)

19. Sunderland were promoted to the First Division despite losing the play-off final because this team were later disqualified for financial irregularities. (7,4)

20. Goalkeeper signed on loan from Blackburn Rovers in 1996 who would go on to win 134 caps for the Republic of. Ireland. (4,5)

Down

2. 1992 FA Cup Final opponents. (9)

3. Sunderland signed Alex Rae from this London club in the summer of 1996. (8)

4. Ex-England player who took over as manager in 1993 but only lasted 65 games. (5,7)

6. Given the number one shirt when Sunderland first started using squad numbers during the 1993/94 season. (4,11)

7. Name of the 6-part BBC documentary series that chronicled Sunderland's 1996/97 season. (7,8)

9. Sunderland bought John Oster from this club in 1999. (7)

10. Shirt sponsor from 1985 to 2000. (4,9)

12. Local lad who scored Sunderland's first-ever goal in the Premiership in 1996. (7,4)

14. Irish forward who scored Sunderland's last goal of the millennia which came away at Old Trafford. (5,5)

15. Side who Sunderland defeated in the 1991/92 FA Cup semi-final. nicknamed 'The Canaries. (7,4)

Round 5 - 2000s

The 2000s started off with back-to-back 7th place finishes. the club's highest in the Premier League to date. They spent seven of the ten seasons in the top division. The best cup run was reaching an FA Cup semi-final which they lost to fellow Division One side Millwall.

Across

2. Sunderland academy product who scored twice on his debut against Crewe Alexandra in a 2004 League Cup tie. (5.6)

4. Succeeded Roy Keane as manager after impressive results as caretaker boss. (5.7)

7. Club whom Sunderland beat in the 2003/04 FA Cup quarter-final. (9.6)

8. National team of goalkeeper Mart Poom who played for the club between 2003 and 2006. (7)

12. Club that Michael Gray joined after 12 years at the club. (9.6)

13. Name of the foundation set up in 2001 by chairman Bob Murray. a play on the stadium's name. (10.2.5)

16. Argentine player who had a cult following at both Sunderland and Middlesbrough. (5.4)

17. Champions League winner who had a successful loan spell at the club in 2008/09. (7.5)

18. Top scorer in the 2003/04 and 2004/05 seasons. (6.7)

19. Top scorer in the 2007/08 and 2008/09 seasons. (7.5)

20. Carlos Edwards scored a stunning long-range winner against this club in 2007 to secure a 3-2 comeback win to put the club on the brink of promotion. (7)

Down

1. Striker who scored the Premier League's first-ever goal and signed for Sunderland in 2005. (5.5)

3. Won the European Golden Shoe in 2000. (5.8)

5. A 17-game losing streak from January to August 2003 was ended when they beat this Lancashire club. (7.5.3)

6. Northern Irish defender who had two loan spells at the club from Manchester United in the mid-2000s. (5.5)

9. Scored the winner against Newcastle in 2008 to secure their first home win in the derby for 28 years. (6.10)

10. Striker signed for a club-record £16.5m in 2009 from Spurs. (6.4)

11. Sunderland secured their Premiership status in the 2007/08 season against this club. (13)

14. Centre-back who scored at the 2002 World Cup before signing for Sunderland the following year. (4.5)

15. Striker signed for a club-record £6.75m from Rangers in 2002. (4.5.3)

Round 6 - 2010s

The 2010s started as a stable Premier League club. After a League Cup Final in 2014. it all went downhill as a few relegation near misses ultimately ended with Championship football in the summer of 2017. Things then got even worse as they finished bottom the following season and once again found themselves in the third tier where they remain to this day.

Across

1. Winger who earned a first-class honours degree in 2015 from Newcastle University whilst playing for the club. (6.7)

2. Scored the winning goal in the dying minutes against Chelsea in the quarter-finals of the 2014 League Cup. (2.4.5)

3. Sunderland's hero in the 2013/14 League Cup semi-finals. saving 2 penalties. (4.7)

6. Sunderland broke the League One Division attendance record in December 2018 in a game against this club. nicknamed 'The Bantams'. (8.4)

8. Vice-chairman and brother of a former Labour Party leader who resigned in 2013 due to the appointment of Paolo Di Canio as manager. (5.8)

12. Sunderland lost to this club in the 2019 League One play-off final. (8.8)

14. Sunderland were beaten by this club in the 2014 League Cup Final. (10.4)

16. Joleon Lescott was signed from AEK Athens in 2017 who are from this country. (6)

17. Left the Wales job in 2017 to become Sunderland manager. (5.7)

18. Signed from Rennes in 2010 after a superb 2010 World Cup with Ghana for a club-record £13m. (7.4)

19. Scored Sunderland's only goal in the 2014 League Cup Final. (4.7)

Down

1. Sunderland announced a commercial partnership with this MLS club in August 2014. (1.1.6)

4. After being named Sunderland's Young Player of the Year for two consecutive seasons. this local lad joined Liverpool in 2011. (6.9)

5. Manager appointed in October 2013. (3.5)

7. The last Sunderland player to make an England appearance. doing so in 2017. (7.5)

9. Sunderland ladies won the Women's Premier League Cup by beating this Yorkshire side in the final. (5.6)

10. Goalkeeper signed from Sint-Truiden in 2010 for £2 million. (5.7)

11. Academy product sold to Everton for £25m in 2017: a record for a British goalkeeper. (6.8)

13. Darren Bent was sold to this club in January 2011 for a then club-record £24m. (5.5)

15. Name of the popular Netflix series which followed the club. Sunderland ___ _ ___. (3.1.3)

The 2020s have not got off to a great start as the Black Cats find themselves in League 1 after failing in the play-offs for a second time in three years in 2021. One bright light was a first EFL Trophy victory at Wembley. but the priority remains getting back into the Championship asap.

Across

4. Midfielder signed from Hartlepool for an undisclosed fee in 2020. (4.6)

5. Caretaker manager between Phil Parkinson's departure and the arrival of Lee Johnson. (6.6)

6. Player nicknamed "Loch Ness Drogba". (4.7)

8. Club that manager Lee Johnson managed before taking charge at Sunderland. (7.4)

9. Academy product who wore the number 8 for the 2021/22 season. (6.8)

11. National team of Arbenit Xhemajli. (6)

13. Frenchman who became majority stakeholder of the club in February 2021. (5.5.7)

16. Sunderland bought this player in on a free transfer from Huddersfield Town in July 2021. (4.9)

17. Ron-Thorben Hoffmann joined Sunderland from this European giant in August 2021. (6.6)

18. Scored the only goal in the 2021 EFL Trophy Final. (6.5)

19. Scored all four goals in a 4-1 win against Doncaster Rovers in February 2021 (7.4)

20. The club lost the 2021 semi-final playoff against this club. (7.4)

Down

1. Sunderland beat this club to lift the 2021 EFL Trophy Final. (8.6)

2. Top scorer in the 2019/20 season with 11 goals. (5.7)

3. Won the EFL Trophy in his last season as a professional after 131 appearances for the club across two spells. (5.10)

7. Sunderland beat the U21 side of this Premier League team 8-0 in the 2020/21 Football League Trophy campaign. (5.5)

10. Phil Parkinson signed this midfielder from QPR in January 2020. (4.6)

12. Lee Johnson's lost his first game as manager of Sunderland against this club. nicknamed 'The Latics'. (5.8)

14. Australian defender signed from Bristol City in 2020. (6.6)

15. Striker who retired in 2021 after his second spell with the club. (5.6)

Two of Sunderland's great managers are Bob Stokoe and Peter Reid who managed the club for a combined eleven years. Both brought the good times back to the club with Stokoe winning an unlikely FA Cup in 1973 and Reid taking a side at risk of relegation to the third tier to back-to-back seventh place finishes in the Premier League.

Across

2. Stokoe was born in the town of Prudhoe which is in this county. (14)

6. Reid began his playing career with this club whom he made 273 appearances. (6.9)

8. Stokoe was manager at this Cumbrian club for three separate spells. (8.6)

11. Cameroon international who was signed by Reid on loan from Parma in 2002. (7.5)

14. Manager whom Stokoe replaced as caretaker in 1987. (8.8)

17. Reid was one of the England players left behind by this player at the 1986 World Cup as he scored the 'Goal of the Century'. (5.8)

18. Club that Reid won two First Division titles and an FA Cup with as a player. (7)

19. Reid's city of birth. (9)

20. Reid's last job in English football was this side. nicknamed 'The Pilgrims' with whom he auctioned off his FA Cup runners-up medal to pay the electricity bill. (8.6)

Down

1. Striker whom Stokoe signed from West Ham who would go on to score 57 league goals in 142 games for the club across two spells. (3.6)

3. Reid was appointed caretaker manager of Leeds United in March 2003 to replace this former England manager. (5.8)

4. Reid was challenged by Kevin Moran who played for this club in the 1985 FA Cup Final and became the first player to be sent off in an FA Cup final. (10.6)

5. Stokoe replaced this manager at Blackpool who is the only man to score a Wembley FA Cup Final hat-trick and scored England's first-ever World Cup goal. (4.9)

7. Reid became manager of this Asian national team in September 2008. (8)

9. Stokoe won the FA Cup in 1955 as a player with this club. (9.6)

10. Stokoe's Sunderland defeated Leeds in the 1973 FA Cup final who were managed by this man. (3.5)

12. Stokoe won the 1971 Anglo-Italian Cup with this Lancashire club after beating Bologna in the final. (9)

13. Reid began his managerial career at this club. nicknamed 'The Citizens'. (10.4)

15. Striker signed by Stokoe from Luton who scored in the 1973 FA Cup semi-final against Arsenal. (3.5)

16. Club nicknamed 'The Shakers'. who were Stokoe's last as a player and first as a manager. (4)

The club have had many other managers through the decades with varying degrees of success. How many of these men can you remember based on these clues?

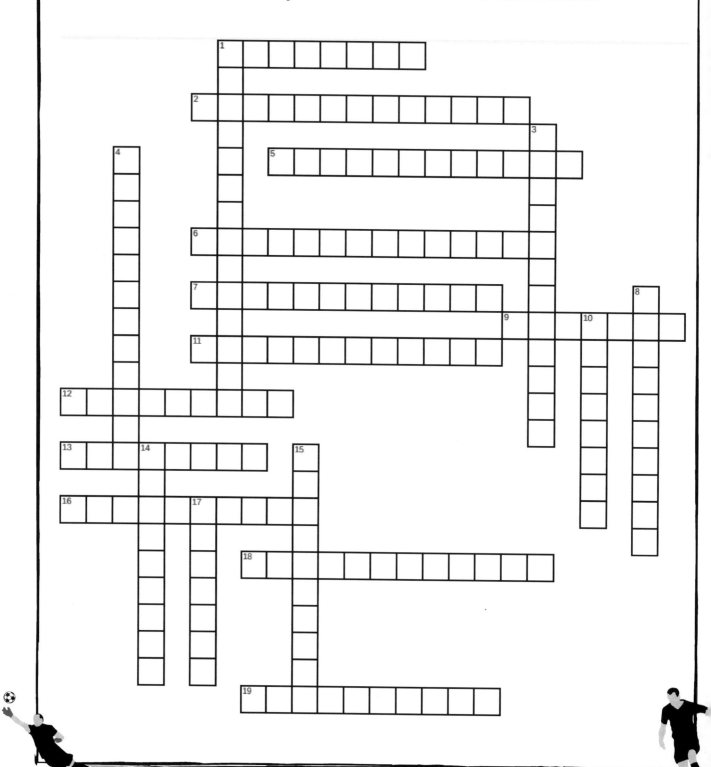

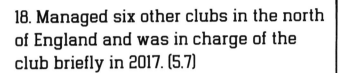

Across

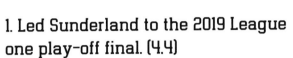

1. Led Sunderland to the 2019 League one play-off final. (4.4)

2. Former Bolton manager appointed in 2019. (4.9)

5. Veteran Dutch manager who was appointed in March 2015. (4.8)

6. Replaced Tom Watson as manager in 1896 to become the second manager in Sunderland's history. (6.8)

7. In charge when Sunderland were relegated to League One in 2018. (5.7)

9. Gus Poyet's country of birth. (7)

11. Famously dropped onto his knees at St James' Park celebrating one of Sunderland's three goals that day. (5.2.5)

12. In 1995. Sunderland was at risk of returning to the third tier of English Football but this manager was brought in and results quickly improved. (5.4)

13. He was named as manager after the takeover by the Drumaville Consortium in 2006. (3.5)

16. The second man to manage both Sunderland and Newcastle. (5.5)

18. Managed six other clubs in the north of England and was in charge of the club briefly in 2017. (5.7)

19. Twice played for teams managed by his father. Gary. (3.7)

Down

1. Won Sunderland their sixth league title in the 1935/36 season. (6.8)

3. Saved the club from relegation in the 2015/16 season. (3.9)

4. Former Ireland manager who took over in 2003. (4.8)

8. Won the 2003. 2005 and 2009 League Managers Association Manager of the Year (5.5)

10. Led Sunderland to the 2014 League Cup final. (3.5)

14. Club legend who was twice caretaker manager in 2006 and 2013. (5.4)

15. Manager that led Sunderland to win their fourth league title in 1902. (4.6)

17. Under this Irish manager Sunderland won the 1912/13 league title. (3.4)

This round is all about the man named as the Black Cats' "Player of the Century" by their fans on the occasion of the club's centenary in 1979. The legendary centre-half scored 23 goals in 402 appearances across twelve seasons for the club ranking him in the top 10 of all-time appearance holders.

Across

3. Hurley turned down this arch-rival of Millwall before signing for them. (4.3.6)

4. His nickname among Sunderland fans. (3.4)

5. Greater Manchester club Hurley joined after leaving Sunderland. (6.9)

6. In a game at Old Trafford in November 1966. Hurley had to play in goal after an injury to this keeper. (5.10)

7. His best run in the FA Cup was the quarter-finals where they were beaten by this team who went on to become the first double winners of the 20th century. (9.7)

8. This London club tried to sign Hurley for £20,000 in 1958. (7)

12. He represented a London XI as they beat this German team to lift the 1955/56 Inter-City Fairs Cup. (9.9)

17. He scored an own goal in a disastrous debut for Sunderland in a match they lost 7-0 to this club. nicknamed 'The Seasiders'. (9)

18. He made his international debut in a match against England and he was supposed to mark this English player who later died in the 1958 Munich Air Disaster. (5.5)

19. Former Sunderland manager who said Hurley was his idol growing up. (6.6)

20. In his youth. he survived this German bombing campaign of Britain. in which one of his best friends was killed. (3.5)

Down

1. National team he represented. (8.2.7)

2. His first goal for Sunderland was against this Yorkshire club. (9.6)

9. One of Hurley's most memorable moments for Sunderland was scoring against this Norfolk side in the 1960/61 FA Cup fifth round. (7.4)

10. Sunderland captain who first suggested that Hurley should go up the field for corners. a tactic that is used by most centre-backs today. (4.8)

11. Manager who signed Hurley for Sunderland. (4.5)

13. City he was born in. (4)

14. He finished second to this West Ham and England centre-back for the 1963/64 FWA Footballer of the Year. (5.5)

15. He joined Sunderland from this London club in 1957. (8)

16. From 1971 to 1977. Hurley was manager at this club. nicknamed 'The Royals'. (7)

Round 11 - Kevin Phillips

One of the club's modern greats. Kevin Phillips is the club's seventh highest scorer of all-time with 130 goals in 235 appearances between 1997 to 2004. He won the European Golden Shoe after a stunning first season in the Premier League with a 30-goal haul. To date, he is still the only Englishman to win the award.

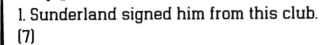

Across

1. Sunderland signed him from this club. (7)

5. He scored a Championship play-off final winner in 2013 for this club. (7.6)

6. When he made his England debut against Hungary in 1999 this Sunderland teammate joined him in the matchday squad. (7.4)

7. He formed a potent "little and large" strike pair with this veteran target man. (5.5)

8. He finished his career winning the Championship title with this club in 2014. (9.4)

10. After his contract with West Brom expired he joined this city rival. (10.4)

11. Phillips' 250th career goal was against this London club. (7)

14. 6ft 7in striker whom Phillips formed another 'little and large' partnership with at Southampton. (5.6)

16. He became the first Sunderland player to score 30 plus goals in a single campaign since this player. (5.6)

17. This manager gave him his England debut in 1999. (5.6)

18. After leaving Blackpool he followed. this manager to Crystal Palace. (3.8)

19. After leaving Southampton he joined this club. (5.5)

Down

2. His first hat-trick for Sunderland was against this Midlands club. (5.6)

3. Phillips started his professional career at Baldock Town who are based in this county. just north of London. (13)

4. He was sent off in a match against Middlesbrough after kicking out at this French defender in 2003. (6.8)

9. This man was the next Premier League player to win the European Golden Shoe after Phillips. (7.5)

10. In 1999. promotion was confirmed in April as Phillips scored four of Sunderland's five goals in an away game against this Greater Manchester club. (4)

12. He was released as a young player by this club who he later re-joined in 2003. (11)

13. He scored a memorable looping long-range volley in a 4-1 win against this side in December 1999. (7)

15. He joined this club after leaving Birmingham. (9)

Round 12 - Roker Park & Stadium of Light

Roker Park was the home of Sunderland A.F.C. for 99 years from 1898-1997. It had a record attendance of 75.118 but finished with a capacity of 22.500. It also hosted four matches at the 1966 World Cup. The club moved to the new Stadium of Light in 1997 which had a capacity of 42.000 that has since been expanded to 49.000. Both grounds have hosted many great Sunderland games as well as England internationals.

Across

1. Irishman who was the first player to be sent off at the Stadium of Light. (5.7)

5. Dutch opponents in the Stadium of Light's opening game. (4)

10. Georgian who was the first opponent to score at the Stadium of Light. (6.9)

12. Scored a famous winner when Sunderland beat Manchester United at Roker Park and the final goal at Roker Park. both in 1997. (4.6)

16. Club legend who dug up Roker Park's centre circle to be placed in the new stadium after the final game. (7.6)

18. Roker Park's highest attendance in the 1970s was against this club. nicknamed 'The Hatters'. (5.4)

19. The last match at Roker Park was played on the 3rd of May 1997 against this team. (7)

20. Name of the stand that was opposite Roker Park's main stand. (5.5)

Down

2. Scored Sunderland's first ever goal against Newcastle at the Stadium of Light. (5.8)

3. Slogan on the Stadium of Light's north stand. (5.3.4)

4. Roker Park hosted this former nation. led by Josef Stalin at the time. three times during the 1966 World Cup. (6.5)

6. Area of Sunderland where the new stadium is located. (13)

7. Scottish opposition in Gary Bennett's testimonial game at Roker Park in 1993. (6)

8. Left-back who scored Sunderland's first ever home goal in the Premier League. (6.5)

9. First player to score a hat-trick at the Stadium of Light. (5.5)

11. A monument in the shape of this kind of lamp stands at the entrance to reflect the coal mining industry that brought prosperity to the town. (4)

13. Sunderland celebrated the tenth anniversary of the new stadium with a pre-season friendly against this Italian side in 2007: the game was drawn 1–1. (8)

14. Side whose stadium name is the 'Estadio da Luz' which translates to Stadium of Light. (7)

15. American singer. married to rapper Jay-Z. who performed at the Stadium of Light in 2016. (7)

17. In the first-ever game at the Stadium of Light. Sunderland defeated Manchester City 3-2 with the goals coming from Niall Quinn. Kevin Phillips and this other player. (3.5)

The club have produced many great local talents through the decades who have gone on to win many honours throughout the world. Can you name these twenty using the following clues?

Across

2. In 2014, he became the first player since Lionel Pérez in 1998 to transfer directly from Sunderland to Newcastle. (4,7)

6. Became the first academy-produced player to be club captain since Michael Gray but was sold to Hull in 2019. (6,8)

8. California-born midfielder who has made over 180 appearances for the club. (6,5)

10. Surname of the brother goalkeepers Jak and Ben, who both played in Sunderland's academy. (7)

11. Northern Irish left-back who made 175 league appearances for the club over two spells and joined West Ham after both. (6,9)

13. French target-man who left in 2016 after just 3 appearances. (6,7)

16. Goalkeeper who had six loan spells away from the club and has earnt 5 caps for Northern Ireland. (6,6)

17. Attacking player who played in the Premier League for Sunderland, Leeds and Newcastle. (7,7)

18. Goalkeeper who spent 17 years at the club and won the European Cup with Nottingham Forest. (5,10)

19. Represented England at the 2018 World Cup and 2020 Euros. (6,8)

20. Scored 16 goals in the 2018/19 season before joining Bordeaux. (4,4)

Down

1. Striker who left in 2010 after just eight appearances before playing for Leicester, Wigan, Rangers and Derby among others. (6,7)

3. Irish international who went on to make 125+ appearances for Plymouth Argyle, Barnsley and Aston Villa. (5,9)

4. Centre-back who made just one appearance for the club and went on to play for Hartlepool, Plymouth Argyle and Motherwell among others. (5,7)

5. Former Scotland international striker who played for the club between 2000 and 2006. (5,4)

7. Midfielder who made over 400 appearances for the club in the 50s and 60s. (4,8)

9. In October 2008, he scored a 25-yard goal against Arsenal and celebrated in emotional style, as he ran over to his manager and had his head on the floor, nearly in tears. (5,9)

12. Made 10 appearances for the club before joining Norwich on a four-year deal in 2020. (4,5)

14. Former Sweden U21 international who made 33 appearances for the club before joining Swansea in 2018. (4,5)

15. Irish international centre-back best known for his time at Sheffield United where he played Premier League football between 2019 and 2021. (4,4)

How well do you know the careers of players outside their time at Roker Park or the Stadium of Light? Here are twenty players based on the permanent clubs they've played for and the period they represented the Black Cats.

Across

3. CS Sfaxien → Lorient → Sunderland (2016-18) → Guingamp → Dijon (6.5)

5. Mallorca → Barcelona C → Barcelona B → Sunderland (2006-09) → Atlético Baleares → Manacor (5.5)

7. Sunderland (1987-98) → Queens Park Rangers (7.3)

10. Newcastle → Cardiff City→ Sunderland (2007-09) → Cardiff City → Ipswich Town → Blackpool → Kerala Blasters → Alloa Athletic → Kerala Blasters (7.6)

12. PSV → Barcelona → Chelsea → Middlesbrough → Liverpool → Marseille → Sunderland (2009-11) (9.6)

14. Arsenal → Bristol City → Newcastle → Manchester United → Blackburn Rovers → Fulham → Manchester City → Portsmouth → Sunderland (2007-08) → Nottingham Forest (4.4)

15. Manchester United → Sunderland (2007-12) → Fulham → Aston Villa → Cardiff City (6.10)

17. Arminia Bielefeld → Borussia Dortmund → Bayern Munich → Sunderland (1999-2000) (6.6)

18. ASEC Mimosas → Beveren → Arsenal → Galatasaray → Sunderland (2016) (8.5)

19. Manchester United → Sunderland (2011-18) → Reading (4.5)

20. Celtic → Spartak Moscow → Everton → Sunderland (2017-present) (5.7)

Down

1. Manchester United → Preston North End → Leeds United → Fulham → Sunderland (2008-11) → Rangers → Bury (5.5)

2. Bastia → Bordeaux → Sunderland (2016-18) → Saint-Étienne (5.6)

4. Luton Town → Waterford United → Sunderland (2005-10) → Celtic → Ipswich Town → Newcastle → Nottingham Forest → Bolton Wanderers → Waterford United (5.6)

6. Stoke City → Sunderland (1983-84) → Everton → Sunderland (1989-92) → Newcastle United → Sunderland (1995-97) → Fulham (4.9)

8. Sunderland (1975-86) → Norwich City → Blackpool → Colchester United → Albany Capitals (5.7)

9. Motherwell → Everton → Birmingham City → Everton → Sunderland (2012-13) → Motherwell → St Johnstone → Motherwell → Queen of the South (5.8)

11. Arsenal → Birmingham City → Sunderland (2011-17) → Hull City → AIK (9.7)

13. Oxford United → Sunderland (2004-09) → Stoke City → Middlesbrough → Huddersfield Town (4.9)

16. Metz → Fulham → Manchester United → Everton → Tottenham Hotspur → Sunderland (2012-13) → Lazio (5.4)

Round 15 - Niall Quinn

Niall Quinn is not only known for his time on the pitch but also off it. After a highly successful period as a player. where he scored 69 goals in 220 appearances. he held roles as chairman. director and even a short spell as manager. He has frequently spoke of his love for the city and the club which is reciprocated by the Sunderland faithful.

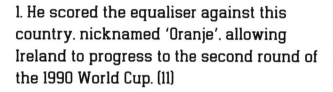

Across

3. His goalscoring record for Ireland was later surpassed by this player in October 2004. (6.5)

6. He struggled to get into the Arsenal side after they signed this target man from Leicester in 1987 who is also a co-commentator for the FIFA video game. (4.5)

9. In a bid to reduce the wage bill. Manchester City tried to sell him to this Portuguese club in 1995 but the move fell through after failing to agree on contractual terms. (8.6)

12. His only victory as manager of Sunderland was against this Midlands club. (4.8.6)

15. He played in goal for Sunderland once which was against this club in 1999. (8.4)

16. This goalkeeper arrived from Manchester United in the same summer as Niall Quinn for £600,000. (4.5)

18. Manager who he surprisingly appointed after stepping down himself in 2006. (3.5)

19. Sunderland manager when he made his last appearance for the club. (6.9)

20. Sunderland signed him from this club. (10.4)

Down

1. He scored the equaliser against this country. nicknamed 'Oranje'. allowing Ireland to progress to the second round of the 1990 World Cup. (11)

2. This club had two bids for Quinn rejected in 1993. (7)

4. Replaced him as chairman of Sunderland in October 2011. (5.5)

5. He made a single appearance for Tero Sasana in 2006 who is from this Asian nation. (8)

7. He scored a famous winner against this club on the 25th of August 1999. (9.6)

8. Goalkeeper who he had to replace in 1999 after he got injured. (6.8)

10. Irish sport he played after retiring from association football. (6.8)

11. He scored twice on his Sunderland debut against this club. (10.6)

13. He scored against this Mediterranean island country on his 35th birthday to break Ireland's all-time goalscoring record. (6)

14. He made his professional debut at this club who he won the 1987 League Cup with. (6)

17. He had an unsuccessful trial at this London club in the early 80s. (6)

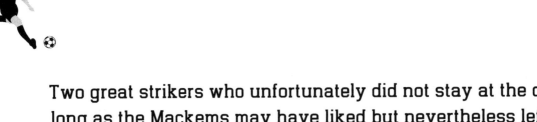

Two great strikers who unfortunately did not stay at the club as long as the Mackems may have liked but nevertheless left their mark. They scored a combined 73 goals in 156 appearances across just five seasons which included many memorable moments.

Across

2. Bent famously scored against this club on the 17th of October 2009 after his strike rebounded off a beach ball. (9)

5. Club that Defoe joined after leaving Sunderland. (11)

8. Defoe scored his sole England hat-trick against this country in 2010, famous for producing former teammate Dimitar Berbatov and Hristo Stoichkov. (8)

10. Bent scored his first England goal after coming on for this striker. (7,5)

13. Club with whom Defoe won his first and only top division title. (7)

15. Club that Bent joined for £2.5m in 2005 and Defoe played for as a youth. (8,8)

17. Defoe's most famous Sunderland goal was a stunning 22-yard volley against this club on the 5th of April 2015. (9,6)

18. Defoe scored his first goal for Sunderland on his home debut against this Lancashire club. (7)

19. MLS side that Sunderland signed Defoe from. (7)

20. Bent progressed through the youth system of this club, nicknamed 'The Tractor Boys'. (7,4)

Down

1. Both men were born in this city. (6)

3. Goalkeeper who Bent scored the infamous beach ball goal against. (4,5)

4. The other club that both men played for. (9,7)

6. Bent scored two goals against this club on his Charlton debut. (10)

7. Whilst playing for Sunderland, Defoe befriended this terminally ill six-year-old fan with whom he formed a special relationship. (7,6)

9. Defoe joined Sunderland in January 2015 in a player exchange deal that sent this striker the other way. (4,8)

11. Club that Bent finished his career at, nicknamed 'The Rams'. (5,6)

12. Defoe scored five Premier League goals in one half against this team. (5,8)

14. Defoe scored his sole goal at a major tournament against this side at the 2010 World Cup. (8)

16. Both men are teetotal which is abstinence from this. (7)

Round 17 - Gary Owers & Marco Gabbiadini

Two club legends of the 80s and 90s are midfielder Gary Owers and striker Marco Gabbiadini. Owers made 320 appearances scoring 25 goals across eight seasons with Gabbiadini scoring 87 goals in 156 games. Owers was part of the team that reached the 1992 FA Cup Final and Gabbiadini's finest season was in 1989/90 as his 21 league goals fired Sunderland into the First Division.

Across

4. Gabbiadini's only season in the Premier League was for this Midlands club. (5,6)

7. Player who went the other way in Owers transfer from Sunderland. (6,5)

10. Gabbiadini scored his first goals for Sunderland against this club. nicknamed 'The Cottagers'. (6)

11. Owers was briefly assistant manager to this former Sunderland manager at Gateshead in 2015. (7,6)

12. Gabbiadini was signed by Crystal Palace as a replacement for this Arsenal bound striker. (3,6)

14. Owers was signed for Notts County by this manager who went on to manage Sunderland in the 2010s (3,9)

17. Owers' last managerial job was from 2017 to 2018 at this club on the 'English Riviera'. (7,6)

18. Gabbiadini is most fondly remembered for. the 2nd in a 2-0 win over this side on the 16th of May 1990. in the play-off semi-final. (9,6)

19. City that Owers was born in. (9)

20. In order for Denis Smith to raise funds to sign Gabbiadini for Sunderland. he had to sell this midfielder who was one of Sunderland's most popular players to Sheffield Wednesday. (4,7)

Down

1. Gabbiadini scored a hat-trick and was then sent off against this side in March 1989. (7,4)

2. Owers played in this position for the 1992 FA Cup Final. (5,4)

3. City. famous for its Roman baths. where Owers had a spell as a player and two as manager ____ City. (4)

5. Gabbiadini formed a strike partnership with this player that was named 'The G-Force'. (4,5)

6. Owers left Sunderland to join this club in 1994. (7,4)

8. Gabbiadini's father is from this country. (5)

9. Owers was the first-team coach at this club who are the most southerly and westerly League club in England. (8,6)

13. Owers made his debut for the club as an 18-year-old in this manager's first game in 1986. (5,5)

15. Gabbiadini had a short spell at Panionios in 1997 who are from this country. (6)

16. Owers made his Sunderland debut against this club. who played at Griffin Park until 2020. (9)

Round 18 - General I

You've done well to reach this far. here are
three rounds of general rounds with questions
from a variety of topics to finish off. good luck!

Across

3. Only West Ham in 1980 and this club have equalled Sunderland's achievement of lifting the FA Cup while playing outside the top tier. (11)

4. Club record signing in 1999 who had a "Space Clause" inserted in his contract, which stated that if he were to travel into space his contract would become wholly invalid. (6,7)

6. Sunderland shares a good rapport with this Dutch club who also play in red and white. (9)

9. Centre-back who was Sunderland's Player of the Year for the 2007/08 season. (5,7)

11. Former player who was appointed manager of Sheffield United in 2021. (4,13)

13. Sunderland's first home ground. (4,5,5)

14. Sunderland fan John Lowe is a three-time world champion at this sport. (5)

16. Sunderland's nickname. (5,4)

17. The historical nickname of Sunderland supporters. (7)

18. Goalkeeper signed in 2007 for £9 million (then the British transfer record fee for a goalkeeper). (5,6)

19. One of the earliest football paintings in the world. Thomas MM Hemy's Sunderland v _____ _____, 1895 depicts the two most successful clubs of the decade. (5,5)

Down

1. An FA Cup 4th Round match against this Somerset club in 1949 is notable for being one of the few occasions in FA Cup history where a non-league club has defeated a top tier team. (6,4)

2. Player who provided assists for all four goals in a 4-1 win against Doncaster Rovers in February 2021. (5,7)

3. Sunderland AFC shared a rivalry with this now-defunct club in the 1880s and 1890s. (10,6)

5. Carlos Edwards and Grant Leadbitter signed for this club for a combined £4m in 2007. (7,4)

7. Legendary Newcastle forward who. supported and made two guest appearances for Sunderland during WWII. (6,7)

8. Player who said that the Tyne-Wear derby was bigger than the Milan derby having played in both. (4,5)

10. Top scorer in the 1894/95 Football League season. (4,8)

12. Holds the record for the most goals scored in a single season for Sunderland with 43 goals in the 1928/29 season. (4,8)

15. The name of the male mascot. (6)

Round 19 - General II

37

Across

5. A popular song sung by supporters is 'Can't Help Falling in Love' by this artist. (5.7)

6. Sunderland has an affiliation with this South African club. (7.4)

7. Nickname for the club whilst they played at Roker Park. (9)

8. Sunderland's goalkeeper when they won the 1937 FA Cup final. (6.6)

10. National team of Lynden Gooch. (6.6)

11. Liverpool manager who signed Jordan Henderson. (5.8)

13. Sunderland signed this defender from Gillingham on a free transfer in 2005. (5.9)

14. Loanee from Manchester United who won Sunderland's 2007/08 Young Player of the Season award. (5.5)

16. Top scorer for the 2006/07 season. (5.8)

18. Matches between Sunderland and this club are known as the "Friendship Trophy". (7.4)

19. Scored a brace against Birmingham to send Sunderland into the 2003/04 FA Cup quarter-finals. (5.5)

20. Fans sometimes sing a version of this song during games, considered a socialist song. (3.3.4)

Down

1. Brand of car that Michael Gray turned up in after relegation for which he was fined 2 weeks wages. (7)

2. Name of the club's fanzine. (1.4.7)

3. This Australian scored the winner for Millwall to knock out Sunderland from the 2003/04 FA Cup at the semi-finals stage. (3.6)

4. The name of Sunderland's female mascot. (7)

9. Mark Proctor made 117 league appearances for the club in between two spells at this North East rival. (13)

12. Sunderland replaced this Staffordshire club when they became the first non-founding club to win admittance into the Football League in 1890. (5.4)

15. Sunderland set up an official supporters club in this communist Asian country in 2019. (5.5)

17. Nationality of former goalkeeper Thomas Sørensen who famously saved an Alan Shearer penalty at St James' Park. (6)

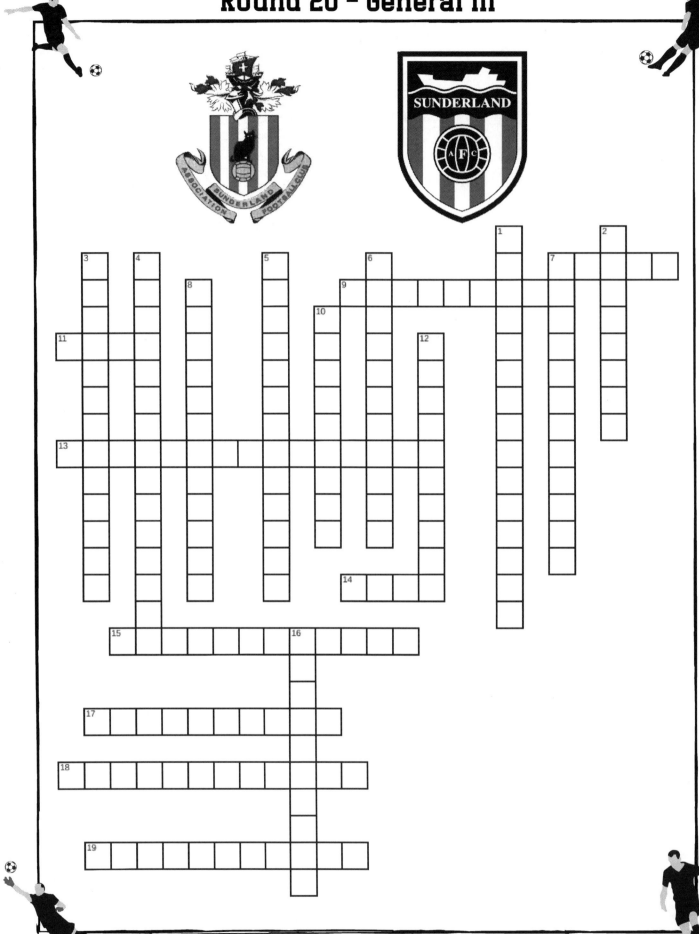

Across

7. Fans launched a campaign to get 'Things Can Only Get Better' by this group back into the charts. to coincide with their team's 2014 League Cup Final. (1.4)

9. Hard-man Albanian midfielder. (5.4)

11. Kit manufacturer from 2000 to 2004. (4)

13. Former England and County Durham cricketer who is a big Sunderland fan. (4.11)

14. The name of the derby between Sunderland and Middlesbrough is called the Tyne-____ Derby. (4)

15. Sunderland's striker whom John Terry said was probably the "best in the air" in the Premier League" after Chelsea had won the match 1-0 on 15 March 2008.. (7.5)

17. Midfielder signed from Blackburn Rovers in 2021 after seven seasons at the club. (5.5)

18. Midfielder who was one of three Sunderland players in the 2002 Irish World Cup squad. (5.7)

19. Famous fan best known for The Eurythmics. his musical partnership with Annie Lennox. (4.7)

Down

1. Sunderland striker who won his sole England cap in 2012. (7.8)

2. Shirt sponsor from 2000 to 2007. (3.5)

3. Outside-left who made over 120 appearances for the club. won 7 caps for England and once scored twice against Brazil in 1956. (5.8)

4. Frenchman who once double nutmegged James Milner at the Stadium of Light. (5.10)

5. Borussia Dortmund and US wonderkid who was born in Sunderland. (8.5)

6. Shirt sponsor from 2007 to 2010. (11)

7. Striker who earned one of his 42 England caps whilst on loan at Sunderland in 2011. (5.7)

8. Sunderland player who captained the United States at the 2002 World Cup. (7.5)

10. Scored an injury-time winner against Manchester City at the Stadium of Light on New Year's Day 2012. (2.4.3)

12. Sky Sports News presenter who is a non-executive director and supporter of the club. (5.5)

16. Centre-back who reached the 2010 World Cup quarter-finals with Ghana whilst contracted to Sunderland. (4.6)

Answers

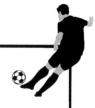

Round 1 - Founding & History

1 PRESTONNORTHEND (down)
2 NEWCASTLEROAD (across)
3 WILLIAMMCGREGOR (down)
4 ARSENAL (across)
5 NEDDOIG (down)
6 NEWCASTLEUNITED (across)
7 JIMMYTHORPE (across)
8 CHARLESTHOMSON (down)
9 IRISH (down)
10 ROKERPARK (down)
11 HEARTOFMIDLOTHIAN (across)
12 DAVEHALLIDAY (down)
13 ASTONVILLA (down)
14 THETIMES (down)
15 JAMESALLAN (across)
16 JOHNCAMPBELL (across)
17 LIVERPOOL (across)
18 BOBBYGURNEY (across)
19 TOMWATSON (across)

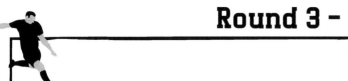

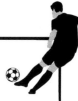

Round 3 - 1970/80s

1 SPORTING LISBON

2 BOBBY KNOX ALL

2 BILLY BREMNER

3 LEEDS UNITED

4 DAVID WATSON

5 JIMMY MONTGOMERY

6 GARY ROWELL

7 NORWICH CITY

8 CLIVE WALKER

9 IAN PORTERFIELD

10 GARY BENNETT

11 GORDON CHISHOLM

12 GORDON ARMSTRONG

13 LEE CHAPMAN

14 BOBBY KERR

15 DAVE MERRINGTON

15 DENIS SMITH

16 HUNGARY

17 LEN SHACKLETON

18 PETER BEARDSLEY

Round 4 - 1990s

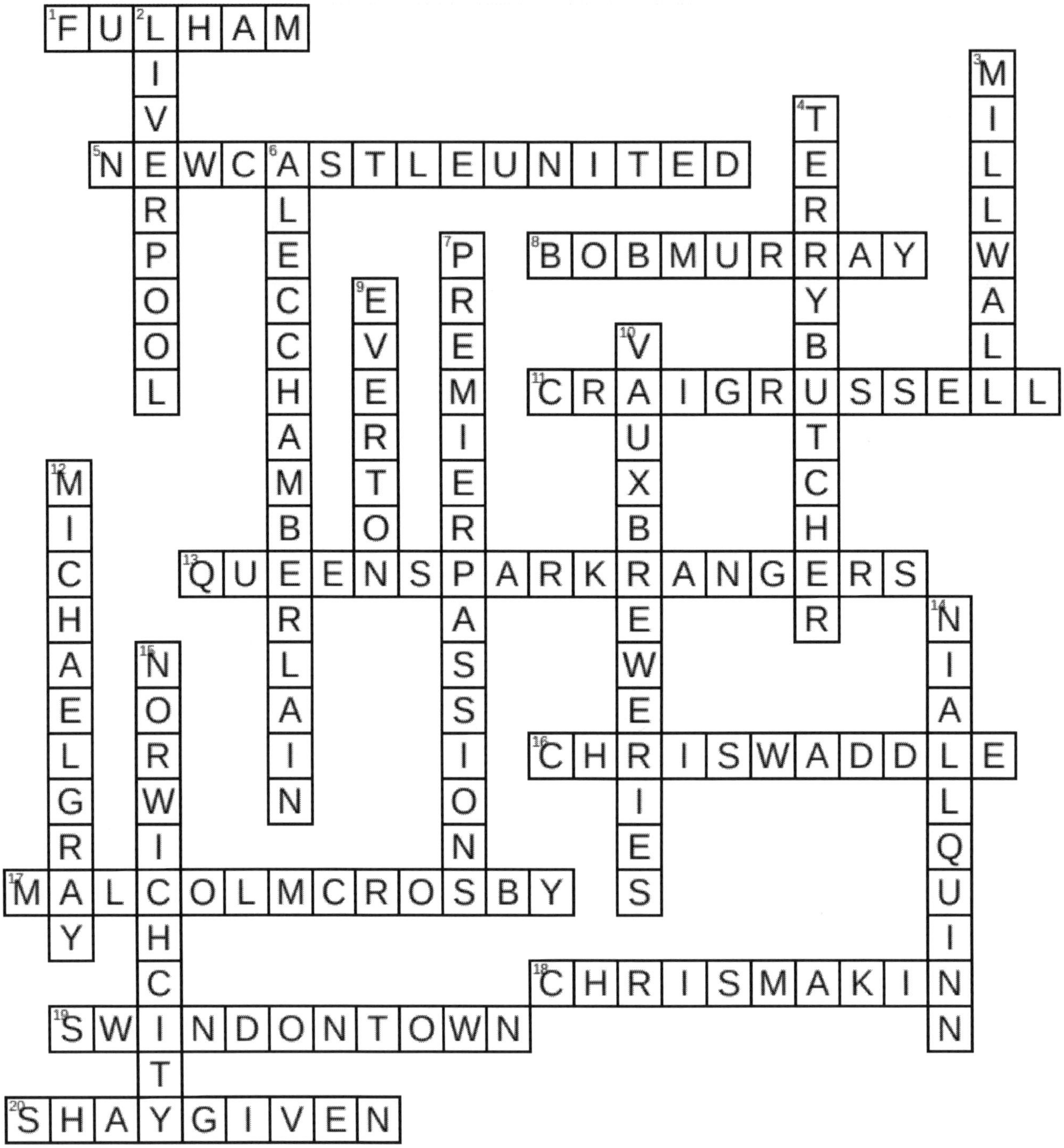
1 FULHAM
2 LIVERPOOL
3 MILLWALL
4 TERRY BUTCHER
5 NEWCASTLE UNITED
6 ALEC CHAMBERLAIN
7 PREMIER PASSION
8 BOB MURRAY
9 EVERTON
10 VAUXBREWERIES
11 CRAIG RUSSELL
12 MICHAEL GRAY
13 QUEENS PARK RANGERS
14 NIALL QUINN
15 NORWICH CITY
16 CHRIS WADDLE
17 MALCOLM CROSBY
18 CHRIS MAKIN
19 SWINDON TOWN
20 SHAY GIVEN

Crossword grid answers:

1. BRIAN (down) — BRIANDEANE
2. CHRISBROWN (across)
3. KEVINPHILLIPS (down)
4. RICKYSPRAGIA (across)
5. PRESTONNORTHEND (down)
6. JONNYEVANS (down)
7. SHEFFIELDUNITED (across)
8. ESTONIA (across)
9. KIERANRICHARDSON (down)
10. DARRENBENT (down)
11. MIDDLESBROUGH (down)
12. BLACKBURNROVERS (across)
13. FOUNDATIONOFLIGHT (across)
14. GARYBREEN (down)
15. TOREANDREFLO (down)
16. JULIOARCA (across)
17. DJIBRILCISSE (across)
18. MARCUSSTEWART (across)
19. KENWYNEJONES (across)
20. BURNLEY (across)

Across and Down answers:

- DUNCAN WATMORE
- KISUNGYUENG
- VITO MANNONE
- BRADFORD CITY
- DAVID MILIBAND
- CHARLTON ATHLETIC
- MANCHESTER CITY
- GREECE
- CHRIS COLEMAN
- ASAMOAH GYAN
- ADAM JOHNSON

Down:
- C UNITE (CUNITE)
- JORDAN HENDERSON
- GUS POYET
- JERMAIN DEFO(E)
- LEEDS UNITED
- SIMON MIGNOLET
- JORDAN PICKFOR(D)
- ASTON VILLA
- ERSON / TILIDIE

Across / Down answers (filled grid):

1. TRANMERE ROVERS
2. CHRIS MAGUIRE
3. GRANT LEADBITTER
4. JOSH HAWKES
5. ANDREW TAYLOR
6. ROSS STEWART
7. ASTON VILLA
8. BRISTOL CITY
9. ELLIOT EMBLETON
10. JOSH SCOWEN
11. KOSOVO
12. KYRIL LOUIS DREYFUS
12. WIGAN ATHLETIC
14. BAILEY WRIGHT
15. DANNY GRAHAM
16. ALEX PRITCHARD
17. BAYERN MUNICH
18. LYNDEN GOOCH
19. CHARLIE WYKE
20. LINCOLN CITY

Across and down entries:

2. NORTHUMBERLAND
6. BOLTONWANDERERS
8. CARLISLEUNITED
11. PATRICKMBOMA
14. LAWRENCEMCMENEMY
17. DIEGOMARADONA
18. EVERTON
19. LIVERPOOL
20. PLYMOUTHARGYLE

1. PROBSON
3. TERRYVENABLES
4. MANCHESTERUNITED
5. STANMORTENSEN
7. THAILAND
9. NEWCASTLEUNITED
10. DONREVIE
12. BLACKPOOL
13. MANCHESTERCITY
15. VICHALOM
16. BURY

Round 9 - Managers

1 JACKROSS

2 PHILPARKINSON

JOHNNYCOCHRAN (down)

3 SMALLALLARDYCE (down)

4 MICKMCCARTHY (down)

5 DICKADVOCAAT

6 ROBERTCAMPBELL

7 CHRISCOLEMAN

9 URUGUAY

10 GUSPOYET (down)

8 DAVIDMOYES (down)

11 PAOLODICANIO

12 PETERREID

13 ROYKEANE

14 KEVINBALL (down)

15 ALEXALEXACKI (down)

16 STEVEBRUCE

17 BOBKYLE (down)

18 SIMONGRAYSON

19 LEEJOHNSON

Round 10 - Charlie Hurley

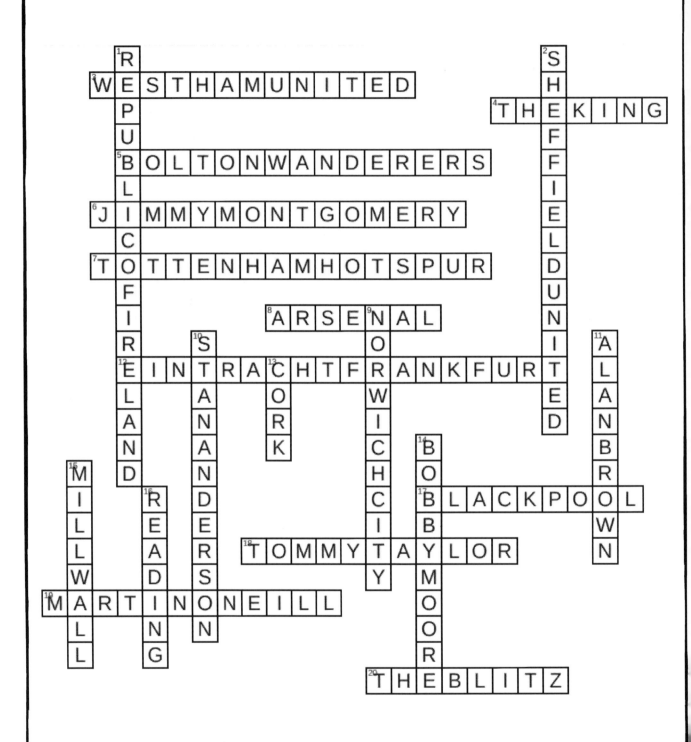

51

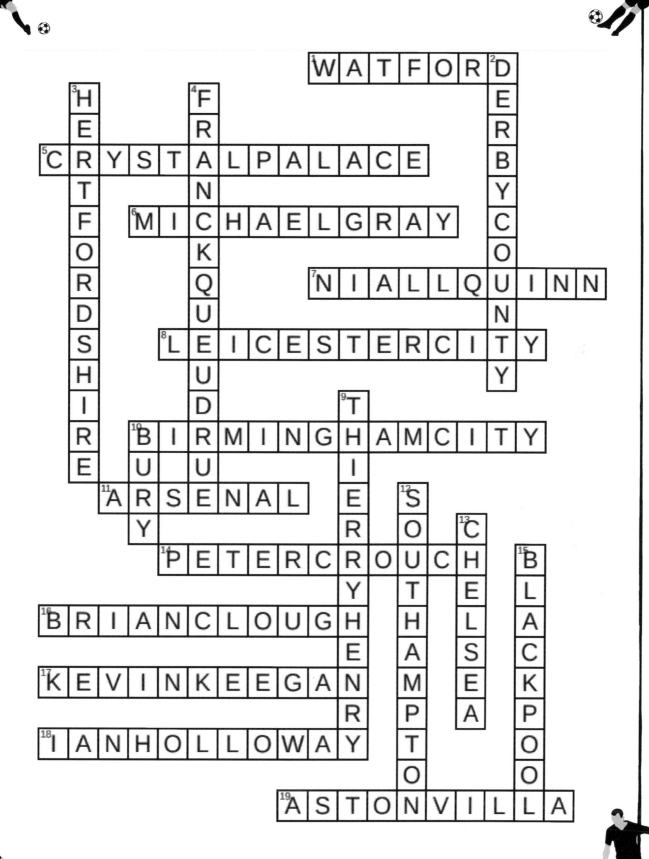

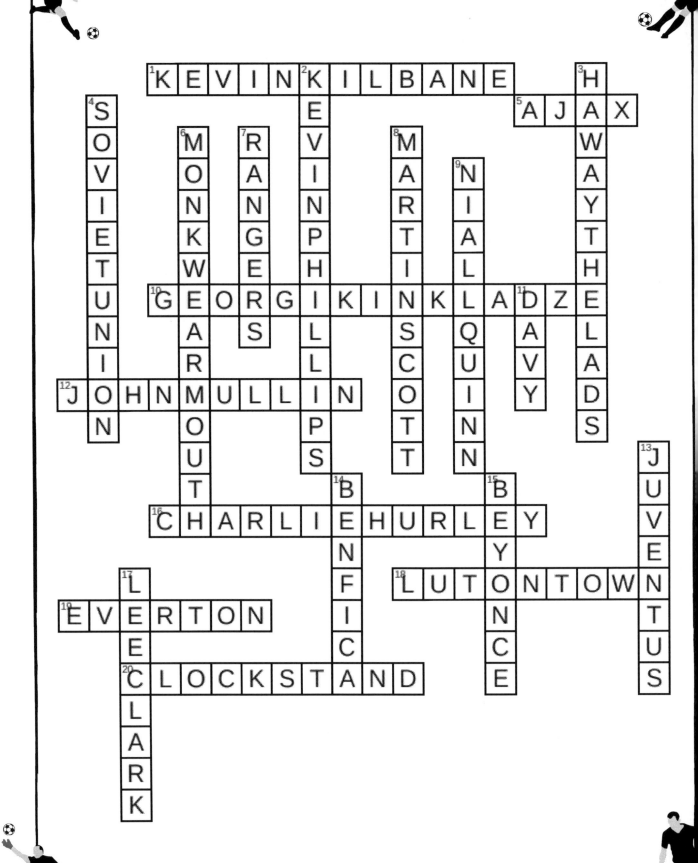

Round 13 - Academy Graduates

Across

2. JACKCOLBACK
6. GEORGEHONEYMAN
8. LYNDENGOOCH
10. ALNWICK
11. GEORGEMCCARTNEY
13. MIKAELMANDRON
16. TREVORCARSON
17. MICHAELBRIDGES
18. JIMMYMONTGOMERY
19. JORDANPICKFORD
20. JOSHMAJA

Down

1. MARTYNWAGHORN
3. CONORHOURIHANE
4. PETERHARTLEY
5. KEVINKYLE
7. STANANDERSON
9. GRANTLEADBITTER
12. BALIMUMBA
14. JOELASORO
15. JOHNEGAN

Round 14 - Career Paths

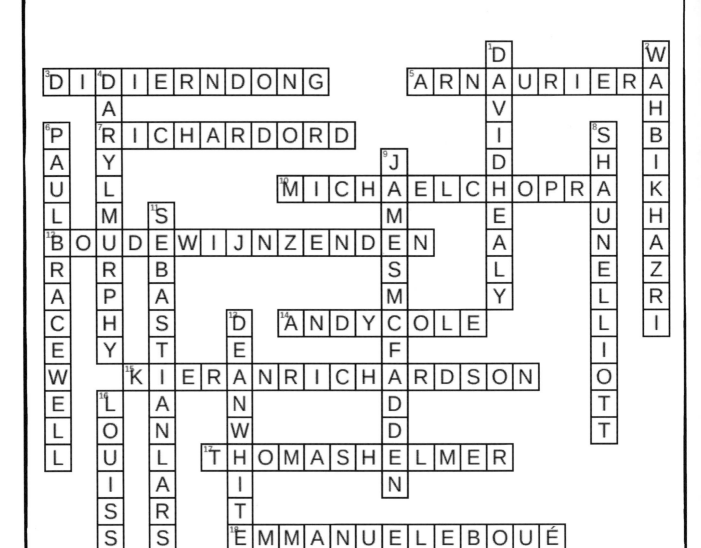

Crossword answers:

3. DIDIERNDONG
5. ARNAURIERA
6. (down) PAULBRACEWELL
7. RICHARDORD
4. (down) DARYLMURPHY
10. MICHAELCHOPRA
1. (down) DAVIDHEALY
2. (down) WAHBIKHAZRI
8. (down) SHAUNELLIOTT
11. (down) SEBASTIANLARSSON
12. BOUDEWIJNZENDEN
9. (down) JAMESMCFADDEN
13. (down) DENNISWHITEHEAD
14. ANDYCOLE
15. KIERANRICHARDSON
16. (down) LOUISSASA
17. THOMASHELMER
18. EMMANUELEBOUÉ
19. JOHNOSHEA
20. AIDENMCGEADY

55

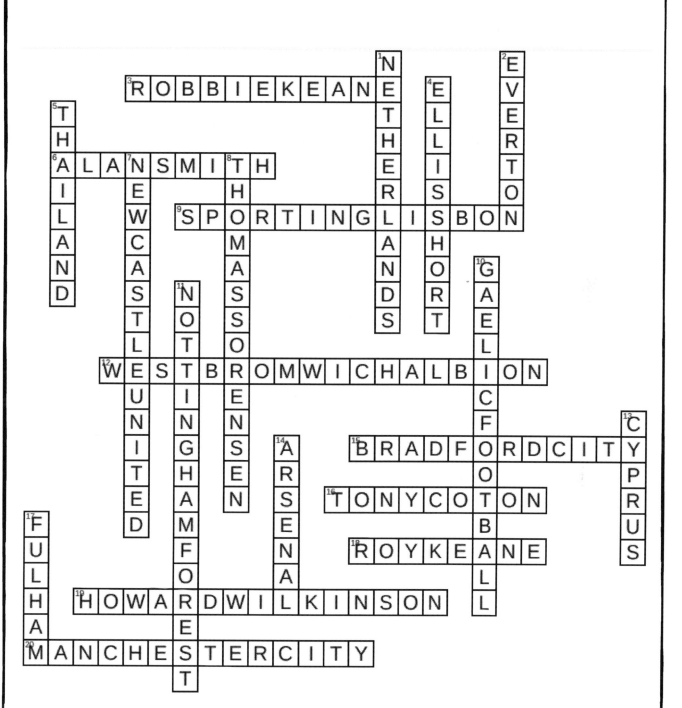

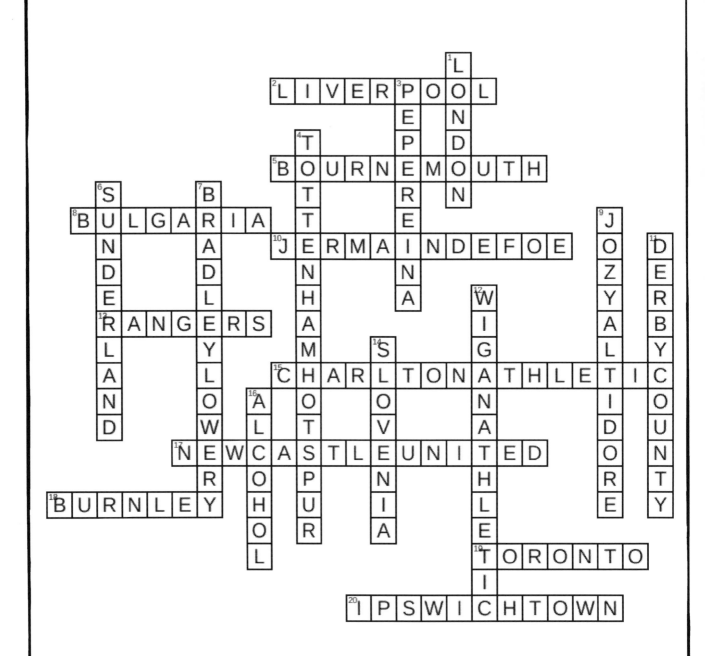

1 LONDON
2 LIVERPOOL
3 PEPEREINA
4 TOTTENHAMHOTSPUR
5 BOURNEMOUTH
6 SUNDERLAND
7 BRADLEYLOWERY
8 BULGARIA
9 JOZYALTIDORE
10 JERMAINDEFOE
11 DERBYCOUNTY
12 WIGANATHLETIC
13 RANGERS
14 SLOVENIA
15 CHARLTONATHLETIC
16 ALCOHOL
17 NEWCASTLEUNITED
18 BURNLEY
19 TORONTO
20 IPSWICHTOWN

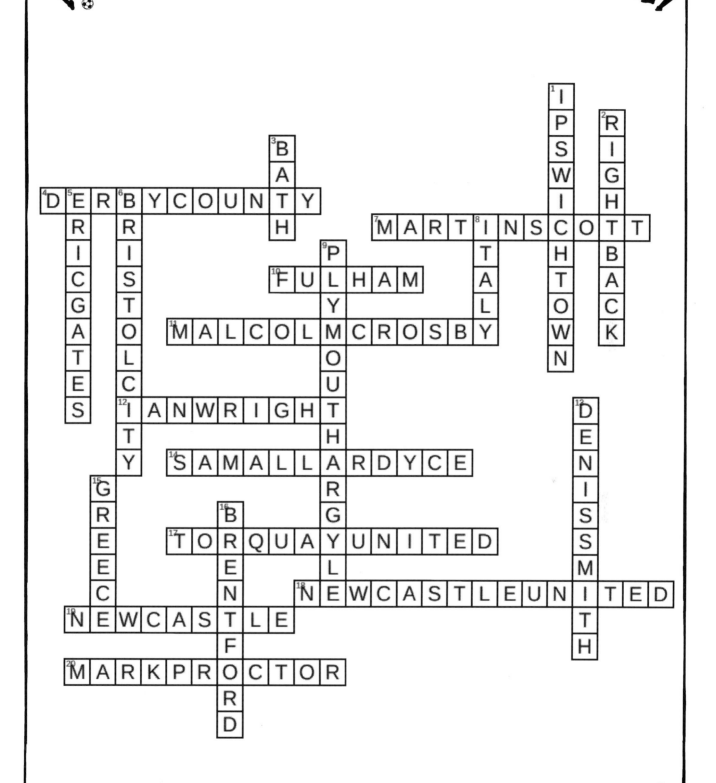

Across:
- 3. SOUTHAMPTON
- 4. STEFANSCHWARZ
- 6. FEYENOORD
- 9. DANNYCOLLINS
- 11. PAULHECKINGBOTTOM
- 12. BLUEHOUSEFIELD
- 14. DARTS
- 16. BLACKCATS
- 17. MACKEM
- 18. CRAIGGORDON
- 19. ASTONVILLA

Down:
- 1. YEOVILTOWN
- 2. AIDENMCGEADY
- 3. SUNDERLAND
- 5. IPSWICHTOWN
- 7. JACKIEMILBURN
- 8. YANNMVILL
- 10. JOHNCAMPBELL
- 12. DAVEHALLIDAY
- 13. ALBION
- 15. SAMSON

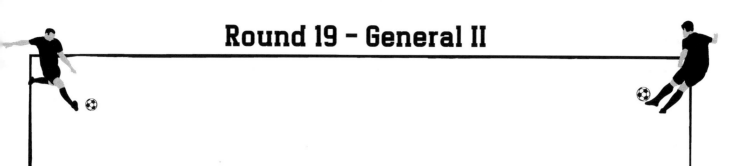

Across / Down entries:

1 FERRARI

2 ALOVESUPREME

3 TIMCAHILL

4 DELILA

5 ELVISPRESLEY

6 BIDVESTBIDS

7 ROKERITES

8 JOHNNYMAPSON

9 MIDDLESBROUGH

10 UNITEDSTATES

11 KENNYDALGLISH

12 NYRONNOSWORTHY

13 STOKECITY

14 JONNYEVANS

15 NORTHKOREA

16 DAVIDCONNOLLY

17 DANISH

18 NORWICHCITY

19 TOMMYSMITH

20 THEREDFLAG

Round 20 - General III

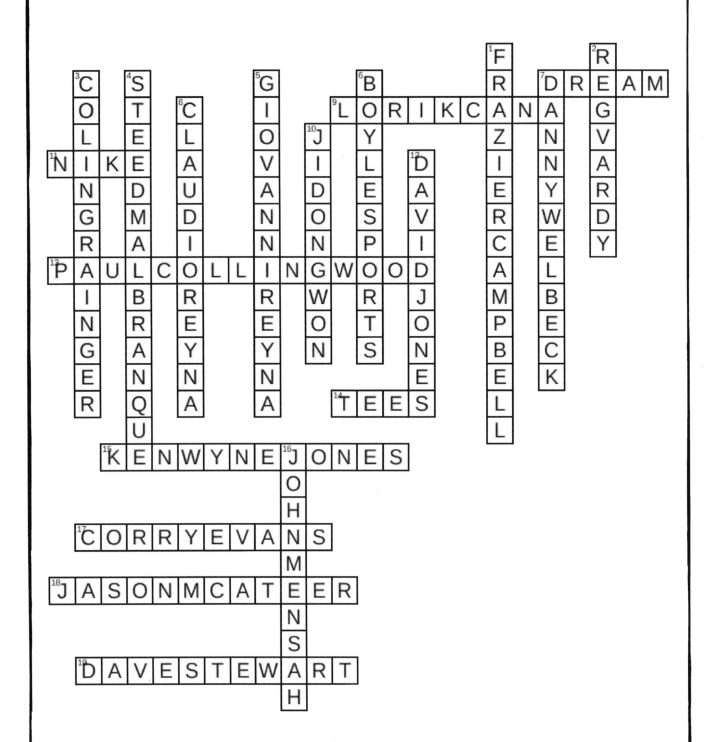

Across and Down crossword answers:

- DREAM
- LORIKCANA
- NIKE
- PAULCOLLINGWOOD
- TEES
- KENWYNEJONES
- CORRYEVANS
- JASONMCATEER
- DAVESTEWART

Down answers:

- FRAZIERCAMPBELL
- REGVARDY
- COLINGRAINGER
- STEEDMALBRANQUE
- CLAUDIOREYNA
- GIOVANNIREYNA
- JIDONGWON
- BOYLESPORTS
- DAVIDJONES
- DANNYWELBECK
- JOHNMENSAH

61

That's all folks, thank you so much for purchasing this Sunderland crossword book. I really hope you enjoyed it and learnt some cool facts about the club to impress your fellow Black Cats.

As a small independent publisher, any reviews you can leave will be a big help as I try to grow my company and produce better and better books for you to enjoy.

If you have any criticisms, please do email me before leaving a negative review and I'd be happy to assist you if you have any problems!

kieran.brown2402@gmail.com

Printed in Great Britain
by Amazon

34330245R00037